# ORDINARY ECSTASY

## Poetry & Aphorism

## Nate Clark

WANDERING PEN PUBLISHING

For all the people I've ever met
and all the people I never will
For all the friends I've loved and lost
and the ones who are here even still

For all the lovers I've ever hurt
and all the ones who have hurt me
For every single tortured soul that
wanders alone by the stormy sea

For the trees and for the rivers
and the infinite stars above
For those who have fallen prey to
the cruel, caring hand of Love

For the drunk with his bottle
For the old man by the fire
For the lonely boy searching
For the bird on the wire

*Poetry is the lovers embrace*

*It is the gaze of the one you love*

*It is sweat on your back*

*and dirt under your nails*

*Your toes find it buried in sand*

*It is in the stars*

*and all around*

*It is infinite*

*as are we*

*Oft called a fool he who*

*polishes brass on a sinking ship*

*but I am like to him*

*Not through a false sense of hope do I polish*

*but rather I know my ship is sinking*

*and I want my last memory of her to be beautiful*

*The sun shone through*

*and for a brief moment*

*everything was bathed in light*

*golden as the first dawn*

*Then the clouds closed in*

*and darkness reigned*

*once again*

*We are whoever we want to be*

*No one can make us be anything*

*The only one with the power to change us*

*is us*

*So be happy*

*or sad*

*or anything else under the sun*

*Be you*

*Be free*

*I dreamed of the summer moon*

*delirious in my bitter recalls*

*The music of the rain*

*sings of whispered sleep*

*Sorrow is the breeze that*

*fills the sail of my heart*

*The night is quiet*

*save for the rustling shadow palms*

*against a sky of ochre clouds*

*and the rain*

*I love the rain*

*Standing outside at night*

*looking to the sky*

*each drop caressing my face*

*like a thousand tiny kisses*

*It is a strange thing*

*the heart*

*Quick to sorrow*

*Quick to joy*

*Tranquility though*

*is difficult*

*The tinkling stream is laughing*

*Whether it laughs at me I do not know*

*If it is, than I laugh with it*

*I know I am foolish*

*It matters not, for I am at peace here*

*The birds are singing, basking in the sunshine*

*that is all too rare in February*

*I bask as well*

*I bask in the sound of the water*

*a poetry too perfect for words*

*It is a strange feeling to miss someone you've never met*

*or to long for something you've never seen*

*a familiar music that you've never heard*

*floats through the air*

*as you breathe in a scent from a childhood*

*that never happened*

*it is strange, for in the midst of these*

*you find yourself, your very essence*

*and you meet yourself for the first time*

*I was alone on an island in a sea of darkness*

*all around me blackest night*

*when I saw afar off a single glistening star*

*It was all I could see in my blindness*

*It rekindled hope in my heart*

*My all, my everything it became*

*My only joy in sorrow*

*My own glistening star*

*The sky is wracked with clouds*

*grey as stone and pregnant with rain*

*Here, now it falls*

*The heavens weep bitterly over a matter*

*too high and lofty and sad for us feeble mortals*

*I understand it not, yet I weep with the clouds*

*and our tears mingle upon the window sill*

*United in our grief we find solace*

*until at last our tears are spent*

*I travel on a journey without an end*

*I travel alone, without a friend*

*I know not where I am going*

*yet I walk on, never slowing*

*Finding joy in cresting each new hill*

*and seeing the earth standing still*

*in the morning.*

*The new, glistening morning*

*But evening comes and I join the mourning*

*of the birds. I bid farewell to the sun*

*and into the night I run*

*Will the dawn ever come again?*

*Will the pale moon ever wane?*

*I walk alone in endless darkness*

*searching for the light*

*buzzed on sadness*

*but not too drunk*

*so much madness*

*but I'm still in love*

*I love memories*

*especially those memories*

*that hurt to remember*

*but would hurt more*

*to forget*

*The power is out*

*Whole block*

*It's okay though*

*I have my guitar*

*my journal*

*and the liquor store is open*


*It's kind of refreshing actually*

*I feel awake for the first time*

*in a long while*


*I was laying in the yard earlier*

*having a smoke*

*The stars seemed clearer and brighter somehow*

*As if the lens had finally been focused*


*The power should go out more often*

*Maybe we would live a little more*

*The full moon shines tonight*

*No creature can hide from her gaze*

*Not even I, though dark my heart*

*Even that deepest crevice*

*is illuminated by her*

*and the world seems less dark*

*The night has no terrors*

*Only beautiful waking-dreams*

*When sleep finally comes*

*I''ll sleep the better*

*for I know She's there*

*Ever-watchful, ever-peaceful*

*A glorious light in the dark*

*I love hotels*

*There is such an intimate*

*relationship with the room*

*though you both know it is temporary*

*It's like a summer fling*

*or a vacation romance*

*Over before it's begun*

*but you never forget it*

*Life is too damn short*

*and too damn long*

*to not do what you love*

*love who you do*

*and just be yourself*


*Fuck it*

*California girls*

*and*

*French wine*

*are*

*all I need*

*maybe*

*some poetry too*

*Drive-ins aren't for watching movies*

*They're for making out in the back seat*

*I miss drive-ins*

*The days blurred together*

*in a wonderful haze*

*of red wine, sex, cuddles,*

*and long midnight walks*

*beneath the moon*

*Strange to think but yesterday*

*my tears watered the ground*

*new peace, new joy*

*I finally have found*

*in you*

*in us*

*I remember when I was a child*

*I used to spin on an inner tube*

*in the pool*

*I'd look through the hole in the middle*

*deep into the watery depths*

*Once I fell off*

*and almost drowned*

*but though I could not*

*tell which way was up*

*and I was swallowing water*

*instead of air*

*I felt that the whole of*

*existence*

*was summed up by the*

*beams of light*

*shooting through the*

*the honey-brew*

*of the pool*

*That's how I feel when I look into*

*your eyes*

*A part of me will live always*

*in the memory of that night*

*we sat on a park bench*

*and talked for hours as*

*the moon sailed across the dark expanse*

*We didn't go to bed until the stars paled*

*and the Sun came up*

*Do you remember?*

*Just a moment is*

*all I ask*

*Don't leave me so soon*

*Even a breathe of a kiss*

*near my lips would be enough*

*Gods watch from above as*

*under the stars I stand watch*

*devils all about me*

*everything paling at the thought of you*

*Lets go to the beach at midnight*

*We can drink whiskey*

*talk to the stars*

*dance with the waves*

*Hell, we could do it naked*

*Rhythm and motion*

*like the swells of the sea*

*I look into your eyes*

*and our souls collide*

*Spirit and flesh mingle*

*We lay entwined*

*We smile, for we know*

*we have touched*

*eternity*

*We're connected*

*you and me*

*by invisible strings*

*incorporeal things*

*that creak like*

*old bedsprings*

*when we end the night right*

*Do you remember that night*

*you and I kissed beneath the fairy lights*

*at a party in December?*

*It was so cold, but you followed me outside*

*when I wanted a cigarette*

*I blew smoke into your mouth*

*and we laughed way too hard*

*Do you remember that night?*

*Do you remember me at all?*

*your black satin dress*

*turned green before*

*my eyes*

*It knew, as I know,*

*that your skin*

*was softer*

*Through your love mine is magnified*

*and beside your beauty I also feel beautiful*

*She is a tropic breeze and a storm*

*a treacherous reef, a haven*

*Her eyes are bright and warm*

*her hair black as raven*

*She sings me to sleep*

*berates me through the day*

*comforts me when I weep*

*She molds me like clay*

*She looked like a mermaid*

*in that teal dress*

*and I stared, stupefied,*

*like a sailor in the doldrums*

*Then she was gone*

*and I was left only with a memory*

*fading fast into shimmering dust motes*

*in the forgotten reaches of my mind*

*I knew then*

*our time would soon end*

*so I soaked up every smile*

*Do not weep, my love, at my departure*

*nor follow me down the path I take*

*for it will be a dark and lonely journey*

*with no moment of respite but my own end*

*Do not wait for me, my love*

*I am drawn inexorably onward and deeper*

*and I will not pass this way again*

*Light no candles for me, my love*

*though I am lost at sea*

*Remember me as I was, and know*

*that I look back on our time together fondly*

*Farewell, my love, farewell*

*"Come to me" she said with a smile*

*I ran towards her, my heart swelling*

*but the air about me turned to salt-water*

*the currents pulled me away and deeper*

*and now in this watery grave I lay*

*my final memory - her sunlit face*

*receding as I drowned*

*Heavy has been my heart*

*and my lips speak only sorrow*

*We've been too many days apart*

*Every night I dread tomorrow*

*It is strange, they say*
*to miss someone who*
*has not yet gone away*
*but I miss you*

*I still smell your scent*
*Still hear your laugh*
*Still feel your warmth*
*but I miss you*

*I miss you, I miss you*
*I should kiss you*
*while I have the chance*
*Before you're gone away*
*and I am left alone*

*missing you*

*I miss all the ways that we were*

*and all the ways that we'll never be*

*I clutch a pillow to my chest*

*pretending it is you*

*but it's not you*

*Nothing*

*No one*

*will ever be you*


*My heart beats fast*

*searching for your heartbeat to match*

*I miss your head on my chest*

*your hair on my lips as I kiss your head goodnight*

*The night is silent and empty*

*without the soft sound of your breathe*


*I miss your warmth next to me*

*I miss you snuggling close*

*I miss the small smile hovering on*

*your sleeping lips*

*I miss holding you tightly and whispering*

*"goodnight, blue eyes"*

*I miss your sleepy, mumbled "I love you"s*

*I miss you, and my bed is cold*

*Linger with me here*

*on the endless spiral*

*of stairs leading from*

*Hell to Heaven*

*We will remain forever*

*alone together*

*in the twilight*

*between the worlds*

*Where now is the summer of youth?*

*Where now the love and the loss, both so sweet?*

*Where now the fervour?*

*Where now the fear?*

*Where now the sleepless nights of feverish planning?*

*Where now the possibilities once so limitless?*

*Where now are you, mon coeur?*

*and where is the damn bottle?*

*Life is an ocean and I am adrift*

*My sails are tattered and sun-bleached*

*I know not where I am*

*nor where I am bound*

*I have no map, no compass*

*I am lost*

*The sea encompasses me*

*and the grey thunderclouds*

*scud by on an invisible breeze*

*so terribly far above me*

*I am adrift on an endless ocean*

*I sat on the beach and watched the sun*

*set below the watery horizon*

*The waves, disregarding the darkness*

*continued to pound and roar*

*A lonely sea gull flew low across the water*

*in the failing light*

*Alighting next to me he let out a last cry*

*I made no move to leave*

*though the darkness was complete*

*So we sat, the gull and I*

*In companionable silence we wore away the night*

*until the sun rose*

*And with a cry of triumph he flew off into the dawn*

*as I waved goodbye*

*The sea calls me*

*The land has made me an outcast*

*a madman and a fool*

*For in my heart I carry*

*a longing for a world that is lost*

*or perhaps never existed*

*They call me dreamer and escapist*

*Why, of course I dream*

*and to escape, I do not deny, I long to do*

*The sea calls me*

*I hear in the sound of the waves*

*no judgement, no mockery*

*I hear whispers*

*and my soul is awakened*

*Whispers of beauty*

*and truth unadulterated*

*by the clamor of society*

*and the din of industry*

*The ocean breeze speaks*

*of joy and hope and peace*

*My spirit longs for the deep*

*The sea calls me*

My board beneath me
The Sun above
Salt-wind in my hair
This is what I love

My toes in warm sand
A rustling palm tree
Beckoning me back
to the bosom of the Sea

But still I go on
I leave Her behind
I'm trapped by "real life"
Until a moment I find

To return to the waves
To set myself free
To live the real "real life"
And finally be
Alive

*In the small hours of the morning*

*I can hear the sea-angels call to me*

*"Come join us!"*

*but I don't go*

*"Leave behind the land!" they say*

*"What has it ever given to you?"*

*I have no answer*

*"You'll never find your sea-legs*

*if you stay ever on the sand!"*

*Perhaps one day I will*

*In line at the liquor store*

*the little girl with her mother in front of me*

*turned and asked me if I had just come from the beach*

*I told her that I had not*

*Looking up at me she smiled and said*

*"Well, you look like you did"*

*I'm standing outside in the garden*

*it's midnight and the stars are out*

*I close my eyes, face tilted towards the heavens*

*I can hear the plants growing*

*their roots splitting the earth*

*slowly, ever so slowly*

*I am bathed in moonlight*

*I am clothed in stardust*

*Perhaps if I don't move*

*I'll grow roots of my own*

*The silver birch sang sweetly*
*as I wandered beneath their boughs*
*lost in memory*
*The silver stream sang softly*
*as I waded through*
*imagining the memories*
*of the water-worn stones*
*The night was all about me*
*alive, not sleeping*

*Nothing ever really sleeps, does it?*
*In dreams, sometimes, we live more fully*

*The morning Sun breached*
*as the Moon hid her beauty*
*once again slipping away*
*at the last moment*
*like a runaway bride*
*Fickle lovers, those two*
*Or perhaps there is a steadiness*
*to love that is ever-pursued, never reached*

*Thus I pondered through the night*

*Oh cease!*

*you woeful tides of time*

*that push and pull, relentless,*

*on the sandy white shores*

*of the human soul*

*Trouble me not with*

*your wearisome prattle*

*you fiend of bitter truth*

*for I have found*

*eternity in this moment*

*and though my body decay*

*and my wits, in time,*

*shall abandon me*

*I'll not die nor fade away*

*No, I will live on always*

*here, now, in*

*the beautiful, the coy,*

*the utterly beguiling*

*present*

*The night is young*

*let us dance naked*

*through the streets*

*for the day is done*

*Now is the time to*

*bask in fever-dreams*

*Let us shake and quiver*

*in our midnight ecstasies*

*Our fervor will illumine*

*the path before our feet*

*and we'll howl at the moon*

*until we collapse*

*limp-limbed and slack-jawed*

*and full to bursting*

*with that wonderful,*

*ethereal substance*

*called joy*

*I laid in the sage and deer weed*
*asking them to swallow me up*
*and set me free*
*I begged them to teach me their ways*
*I was left unanswered*
*I sat by the stream and asked*
*how I might also be so steady*
*I was met again with silence*
*I asked the breeze where it was going*
*and if I might come along*
*Silence*
*I asked the stones to teach me their wisdom*
*Silence*
*I asked the trees to lend me their roots*
*that I too might touch the sky*
*Silence*
*I asked the bees the secrets of honey-making*
*Silence*
*Finally I stopped my querying*
*I leaned against a stump and sat quietly*
*for hours, mourning my own ignorance*
*Eventually I ceased to mourn and was silent*
*I smiled, I stood, and turned my steps towards home*

*I found solace in the company*

*of the bearded palms of the canyon*

*It seemed they too*

*longed for a home that they*

*had never known*

*beauty is the chalice that love fills up*

*so we might be drunk on both*

*I looked to the stars*

*searching for a reason to go on*

*I was surprised when they answered*

*We will never reach tomorrow*

*yet we will never again*

*experience today*

*Even the night is polluted*

*Is anything sacred anymore?*

*I long for the part of me*

*that still wanders in forgotten dreams*

*The world has become full*

*Full of distractions*

*Noise and motion and color*

*assault us on all sides*

*In the chaos of*

*"fulfillment"*

*we find we are empty*

*In a whirl of sensation*

*our souls have been stolen*

*Pain is one of the few constants*

*of the attentive man*

*For when one is not blinded*

*by lies and distractions*

*one cannot help but see all the pain*

*and to feel it intimately in one's soul*

*So many of our creations have*

*become like the world around us*

*Sedated and soulless*

*like a piano with no keys*

*How then does that which*

*gives our greatest joy*

*strike us also*

*with utmost grief?*

*Sometimes more can be said in silence*

*a glance, a smile*

*than could ever be said with words*

*I laid 'neath the shrubbery*

*by the roadside*

*content in my solitude*

*I had found my own small Eden*

*in the depths of the City of Man*

*and the sun rose black*

*a hundred years from now*

*The earth was silent*

*for all of life had been*

*snuffed out by mankind's folly*

*A solitary tree crumbled to dust*

*with no one to mourn it*

*A single, lonely star*

*gave a last glimmer and died*

*then darkness descended*

*complete*

*for the last time*

*If my road leads to Hell*

*I will walk it joyously*

*with no hesitation*

*At least I will be in Hell*

*having lived a life of love and laughter*

*rather than Heaven*

*remembering for eternity*

*that I never lived*

*Our world has become a meaningless void*

*Days filled with meaningless noise and excess*

*In our gourmandizing*

*we don't realize that we gorge ourselves*

*on poisoned fruit*

*The poet has an intimate relationship with sorrow*

*For in his search for beauty he has found*

*that every beautiful thing has its end*

*This does not diminish it's beauty*

*No, the fleeting nature of the object is*

*if not the, then a reason it is beautiful*

*In a world where fear of death*

*has become almost universal*

*anything that threatens our illusions*

*of stability becomes dangerous*

*Fear makes men into beasts*

*but ignoring fear merely hastens*

*the end that men dread*

*When did we forget our ability to create?*

*When did we forget our own immortality?*

*We live through the ages by what we leave behind*

*or we are forgotten, having never realized*

*our power, our potential*

*We are gods, for we, unlike the plants and animals*

*have the capacity to give life*

*to our thoughts and our dreams*

*What were the gods if not creators?*

*What were the gods if not wardens and watchmen*

*of the natural order?*

*How, then, are we any different?*

*We have forgotten ourselves*

*It is past time to remember*

*They call me apathetic*

*because I don't care what people do*

*In truth, though*

*I think I have reached*

*the height of empathy*

*It is only when we cease to care about anything*

*that we are able to begin to care about everything*

*The Christians say we're golems*

*and the Evolutionists, apes*

*I say*

*Who cares? We're alive, damnit*

*The honeymoon phase*

*never ends*

*unless you end it*

*The human spirit is an*

*unfathomable maze*

*If you get bored*

*then you're not searching anymore*

*If you stop searching*

*then you're done*

*If you never go out past the shallows*

*the sea will reject you*

*and you will be forever apart*

*from the endless*

*beauties and mysteries*

*of the deep*

*unexplored regions*

*of being*

*We all stand on the shoulders*

*of those who came before*

*Once we accept that*

*and let go*

*We can touch the stars*

*"Temperance is a virtue"*

*Is it?*

*I'd rather*

*drink too much*

*smoke too much*

*love too much*

*drive too fast*

*sleep too little*

*fight too often*

*and burn out quick*

*than fade away slowly into*

*oblivion*

*That which is touched*

*is that which is polluted*

*but the glistening vision*

*that stays ever just out of reach*

*never fades*

*old-fashioned's and cigarettes*

*don't take the pain away*

*I still have my debts to pay*

*but not tonight*

*ask me again tomorrow*

*maybe I'll have an answer then*

*There! Now that we had performed*

*the quintessential activity of life*

*what do you think about death?*

*Will the soul die with the body?*

*If not, do you think two souls can*

*have sex, sans physical form?*

*Oh, you have to go?*

*Bye*

*The fool who knows he is a fool is wiser*

*than the wise man who knows he is wise*

*To me, sorrow and joy*

*are equally beautiful*

*I love rainy and sunny days alike*

*I love to cry, I love to laugh*

*Heartbreak is as potent*

*as blossoming love in my eyes*

*I want to feel everything*

*to the utmost extreme*

*It's complacency that I hate*

*I looked and saw*

*butterfly breath and*

*rivers of amber*

*the hummingbird*

*on the verge of death*

*yet never so close*

*to life*

*Keep your credit cards*

*and your dollar bills*

*I'll buy my happiness*

*with sea urchins*

*and salty kisses*

*The finiteness of our existence*

*weighs heavy on the heart*

*but the ineffable wonders we might still know*

*outnumber the very stars*

*Stop! Listen! do you hear*

*the infinite song of this earthly sphere?*

*There is not time enough in the day*

*to hear all that Nature has to say*

*The night ends before I learn the crickets litany*

*but hark now!*

*What is this beginning melody within me?*

*I can't help but dance*

*Je suis de la terre*

*Je suis de l'eau*

*Je suis de l'air*

*Je suis du feu*


*Je suis tout*

*All the world is a-thrum*

*with the pulsing, vibratory dance*

*of every atom and particle*

*each in their assigned place*

*forming the mosaic backdrop*

*of the stage on which we perform*

*peel back the veil*

*and look with fresh eyes*

*on the indelible beauties*

*of the soul*

*Let me be as the honey bee*

*flitting about from tree to tree*

*blossom to blossom, flower to flower*

*filling up the intricate walls of my bower*

*with every sweet drop of nectar*

*the world has to offer*

*chasing beauty day by day*

*There is no rulebook for creation*

*no criterion for beauty*

*no treasure map to eternal bliss*

*All we can do is*

*turn over stones, peer at the stars*

*mix colors, pluck strings*

*sing and dance and screw and laugh*

*There is too much to learn*

*too much to explore*

*too much to taste*

*to waste time being petty*

*or righteous or cruel*

*There are many strange brews to drink*

*I'll quaff them all ere I sleep*

*My thirst will not be slaked*

*nor my mind cease to ponder*

*the endless parade of Mystery*

*My feet will always wander*

*the paths I'm told to avoid*

*I will walk into the darkest depths*

*and back again before I am silenced*

*I will sow the seeds*

*of my broken heart*

*the whole world over*

*I will water them*

*with my tears*

*the joyful and sorrowful*

*vintages both*

*What may bloom from*

*these pieces of me*

*I don't know, but*

*all I can hope*

*is that they are*

*beautiful*

*Empty bottles all around me*

*cigarette butts piled high*

*laying on a bed of broken glass*

*I must decide*


*Despair or ecstasy?*


*Suddenly the epiphany strikes*

*and I see the unmeasured beauty*

*of all that I called ordinary*

You can find me at the beach

bumming about, strumming my guitar

scribbling down a line or two as they come

If you really need to find me

just follow your feet

We'll cross paths eventually

Please bring tales of mysterious

and serendipitous events

bring joy and wonder and magic

bring yourself

your real self

or at the very least bring me a beer

I'm sure we'll have a great time

or an interesting one, if nothing else

Stay weird and

chase the indigo night

-n.c.

Wandering Pen Publishing, LLC
San Diego, California


First edition

ISBN 978-0-578-97279-4 (paperback)

CPSIA information can be obtained
at www.ICGtesting.com
Printed in the USA
BVHW071931141021
618959BV00004B/324